Ancient Persian Designs in Needlepoint

27 color plates and 57 graphs

Robert Horace Ross

with Marjorie Ross Reinhardt

Photographs by Edward L. Wintringham

ST. MARTIN'S PRESS/NEW YORK

Design by Manuela Paul

Library of Congress Cataloging in Publication Data

Ross, Robert Horace.
  Ancient Persian designs in needlepoint.

  1. Canvas embroidery—Patterns. 2. Decoration and ornament—Iran. 3. Rugs, Persian. I. Reinhardt, Marjorie Ross. II. Title. III. Title: Persian designs in needlepoint.
TT778.C3R66   746.44′2041   82–5716
ISBN 0-312-03583-7   AACR2

First Edition
10 9 8 7 6 5 4 3 2 1

To my father, Howard,
Marjorie, and John

Acknowledgments

My deepest gratitude to my sister, Marjorie Ross Reinhardt, who stitched twenty-one of the color plates. Without her superb mastery of technique and design interpretation, this collection of needlepoint designs would not have been possible.

Many thanks are due: Narcisse Chamberlain for her guidance, help, and encouragement; A. T. Hannett for critical design suggestions; Don McGee for all his unselfish help; Sam Sternberg of the Pillow Shop for his perfection in finishing the pieces; Sue, of Sue's Needlepoint, for providing the widest range of colored yarns.

About the Graphs and Yarn Counts

For each of the twenty-seven designs, a small-scale, overall graph is presented, followed by one or more graphs reproducing a segment of the design in a larger, more legible scale. These are the stitching graphs. The smaller, complete ones show how the segments fit together.

For bilaterally symmetrical designs, only the right-hand side (the side stitched first) has been enlarged. For maximum ease in following the graphs, the right side has been further divided into upper and lower quadrants. Stitch the upper right one first. To stitch the upper left, work the pattern in the opposite direction from the center line. If you have trouble working the graphs in reverse, you can have a flopped (mirror-image) photostat made and work from that. Dark lines at the top and side of each quadrant indicate the center line. If the center line falls on a stitch, as in all odd-number stitch patterns, work that center stitch only once. It's a good idea to count out the number of stitches for the innermost row of the border—or the outermost row of a solid background, if there is one—to serve as a guide.

For designs that are quadrilaterally symmetrical, only the upper-right quadrant has been graphed. Again, the upper right is stitched first.

Remember that each square on the graph corresponds to a stitch. The grid lines on the graph do *not* correspond with the threads of your canvas.

Unique to this collection is a series of Designer's Companions, each based on a single element of the intricate carpet patterns. The design can be made to any size by increasing or decreasing the number of pattern repeats.

Remember that additional rows of stitching—not always indicated on the graphs—will be necessary on all four sides so that part of the pattern is not lost when the piece is framed or made up into a pillow. Check with your upholsterer or framer, but a good rule of thumb is three to four rows for a pillow, and four to eight rows for framed pieces.

If you compare some of the graphs very closely with the color plates, you may spot some minor changes in the graphs. These are some final adjustments to the original designs, made by the author after the color plates were made.

Wool requirements for these needlepoint designs are measured in strands where one strand of 3-ply Persian yarn is 18 inches long, and roughly 48 strands equal one ounce of yarn. The designs were worked on #10, #12, or #14 interlocked mono canvas. The appropriate number of strands for the canvas size is indicated for each pattern.

Introduction

Oriental rugs are one of man's earliest and finest expressions of creative artistry. They are as old as history; the art of weaving can be traced back to the beginning of civilization itself in Persia. This art form has been accepted and appreciated since its first introduction into Europe at the time of Elizabeth I of England at the end of the sixteenth century, when the doors of Persia were opened to trade with the West. Unlike many other fine art forms, weaving had utilitarian beginnings. Throughout a turbulent history it continued, was developed to a perfection, flourished as an embellishment to luxurious living, and has remained virtually unchanged for centuries.

There is a great beauty in the artistic creations of those unknown, unnamed "great masters" of the East. It is easy to appreciate paintings of the Great Masters, but how different really is the weavers' art? The weavers create an abstract form of beauty, unsurpassed by any other art form, using natural materials that have a sheen and colors that mellow with age.

The taste for beauty is based on convention and the degree of societal cultivation. The aesthetic sense of the peoples of the Orient is cultured to a standard beyond the comprehension of the Western world. The highest expression of genius in Occidental art may be stated in utmost realism; whereas Oriental art depends less on realism and more on suggestive abstractions, which our eye interprets differently at various times. Weaving is an expression of the inner spirit, the harmony of life, the moods of joy, peace, and sorrow. The weaver's creativity reflects nature as well as everyday life where religious thought, philosophy, mysticism, and surroundings are inseparable. Unlike other art forms, weaving is directly related to the climate and terrain that influence the basic design by the use of local wools and natural, native dye sources.

We must understand the weavers, their ways of life, the features of their lands and surroundings, to understand the development to perfection of Oriental rug design. The principal origins of the designs we know today are found in areas of Afghanistan, Baluchistan, Luristan, Turkestan, Persia, Turkey, and the Caucasus. The traditional rug designs of India and China are distinct and not necessarily what we most commonly think of when we say "Oriental rug" designs, hence I have chosen not to represent Chinese and Indian designs.

The geography of the areas of design I shall consider varies greatly through desert wastes, level lands, mountainous terrain, and from brutal cold and wind to the serene, warm, lush, and fertile valleys. In these surroundings works of art are created by nomadic tribesmen, village dwellers, and the more sophisticated city folk.

The evolution of weaving and the development of designs has spanned centuries of turbulence. From the time of earliest recorded civilizations in the Tigris-Euphrates Valley (3500–3000 B.C.) to the founding of Afghanistan in 1747 and the more recent assimilation of Armenia and the other nationalities of the Caucasus into the Soviet Union, no one political or cultural power has remained dominant within any fixed boundary for any long period of time. The rise and fall of nationalist powers, the expanding and contracting of social, cultural, and political influences, the traces of cultural interchange, all helped to formulate, solidify, and create the variety of characteristic designs we know today.

The ability to identify Oriental rugs by their designs adds to one's enjoyment. In identifying them, we may consider pattern, coloration, borders, weave, knots, symbolism, warp and weft materials, wool type, the uses of cotton, linen, and silk, fringe, selvage materials, and webs, nap, and dyes. There are definite characteristics of each design classification group, but an exception to any hard rule can always be found. I have limited my needlepoint interpretations of Oriental rug designs to those elements and colors that are considered basic characteristics and are not contested by the scholars. Rugs were named after the cities in which they were woven, after the nomadic tribes who wove them, or after the cities in which they were sold; sometimes the names were derived from a combination of the above.

Scholars agree on a broad geographical classification of six groups of Oriental rug designs: those from Persia, Asia Minor, the Caucasus, Central Asia, China, and India. In addition to the four broad geographic areas of design I shall interpret, I shall use an even broader classification of Persian designs devised by Arthur Gregorian. This grouping lends itself beautifully to the needs of the less knowledgeable needlepoint craftsman. These three design groupings, regardless of geographic classification, are: geometric or nomadic tribe designs; florals; and conventionalized designs.

Geometric designs may be Persian, Caucasian, Turkestan, Afghan, Turkoman, or Baluchistan in origin. (These groups may be further subdivided.) Geometric design is the expression of the illiterate nomad who wanders with his flock in search of warmth and green pastures. He weaves his creation on the floor of his tent, which limits the size and shape of his design. He is complacent and undisturbed by distraction. He expresses himself with the materials at hand: wool from his animals; dyes from roots, minerals, barks, bugs, and the plants with which he comes into contact. The designs are free, bold, dynamic, and somewhat naive, in pure, primary colors—a contrast to the drab wasteland he may roam. There is no sophistication, no shading, and no preplanning. He creates that which is familiar, what he has seen, and what has been handed down from tribe to tribe, family to family, for generations. Only minor variations to the basic design occur. These are the result of human error, not experimentation. The basic pattern of a region remains a constant personal affair, within the limits of the nomad's cultural contact, local technique, and technology. Typically representative designs are: Afghans, Central Asiatic Baluchistans, Turkoman Bokharas, Persian Bakhtiaris, Caucasian Derbends, Khivas and Kazaks, and the Ladiks of Asia Minor.

PLATE 1

Baluchistan

PLATE 2

Afghan (*lower left*)
Afghan Designer's Companion (*upper right*)

PLATE 3

Bakhtiari *(upper left)*
Kashan *(upper right)*
Tekke Prayer *(lower left)*
Kirman *(lower right)*

PLATE 4

Kazak *(lower left)*
Kazak Designer's Companion *(upper right)*

PLATE 5

Herat *(lower left)*
Herat Designer's Companion *(upper right)*

PLATE 6   Sarouk

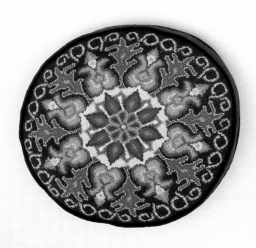

PLATE 7

Afghan *(upper left)*
Baluchistan *(upper right)*
Bijar *(lower left)*
Bijar *(lower right)*

PLATE 8

Bijar *(lower left)*
Bijar Designer's Companion *(upper right)*

PLATE 9

Tabriz *(lower right)*
Tabriz Designer's Companion *(upper left)*

Sarouk Designer's Companion

PLATE 10

Sarouk

PLATE 11

Khiva Bokhara *(lower right)*
Saraband *(lower left)*
Ganja *(upper right)*
Tekke Bokhara *(upper left)*

PLATE 12

Kashan

Floral designs are for the most part Persian in origin. They are the product of the city dweller with his more sophisticated cultural life. They reflect the philosophy, poetry, religious thought, and education of city life, where living is more leisurely and sedentary, and particularly where the space to create larger, more meticulous designs is available. Boldness gives way to intricate detail; shades and tones of colors are further used to express various levels of thought or mood. The designs are always interlaced and delicate and tend toward the realistic. Roses, vines, palmettos, and trees are plentiful. Typical floral designs of this group may be identified by the city from which they come: Sarouk, Kirman, Bijar, Qum, Kashan, Isfahan. Victorian tastes sought out and popularized the Sarouk; more recently the softer shades of the Kirman have become popular.

Weavers of conventionalized design live in the villages surrounding the cities. Their works, like their villages, lie somewhere between the tents of the nomads and the walls of the cities. The designs are less realistic than the city dweller's florals and less angular than the nomad's geometrics. The designs are highly stylized representations of some of the cultural influences touching them from the cities. These weavers' lives are somewhat sedentary, routine, seasonal, and predictable. Their works are repetitious, but the repeated pattern is both soothing and peaceful. Realism is reduced to a stylized suggestion in floral patterns. Typical representations of this group are found in the Persian Saraband, Herat, Senna, Tabriz and Fereghan, Serapi, and some Bijars.

Symbolism plays a great part in the design of Oriental rugs. Thoughts, moods, beliefs, are all translated into the design. Color itself is a symbol: Shades, tones, and intensity of specific colors heighten and lessen the emotion or mood. Green is sacred; blue represents eternity; red conveys joy or happiness. Explanations of the individual symbolic meanings will be touched upon as they are encountered in the designs that I have created for the needlepoint craftsman.

There is a very close correlation between needlepoint and Oriental rug weaving. The materials are the same; both products are extremely durable; each may be a permanent record of a given cultural level of society, outliving the craftsman by hundreds of years. Each piece of art takes proportionately the same hours of devoted labor. There are no shortcuts, only variations in stitches and knots. The desire to produce a permanent, durable work of art of which one can be proud is the same.

The Oriental rug design patterns I have created represent the categories that are most easily identified and with which we are most familiar. I have attempted to create designs that include those qualities of Oriental rugs that are equally adaptable to needlepoint: careful delineation; flowing lines; the balance of the parts as they relate to the whole; a consideration of coloration as related to the group type; harmony of field and borders accentuating the distinct qualities of each. No one rug type or classification is superior to another, although one may appeal more to one's senses and individual taste. Examples of nomadic geometrics, conventionalized designs, and florals are included in this collection representing the artistic achievements of the weavers of Persia, Asia Minor, Central Asia, and the Caucasus.

No design has been created arbitrarily. Each design of this collection has been derived from an existing piece belonging to a private collection, museum, or dealer. No design in the collection has been copied in toto, since converting a room-size rug to needlepoint would be impossible. In some instances, the main medallion (the central, major motif) or one of many repeated patterns has been featured as a central motif. Borders are always representative of the specific design type, although some may have been deleted as a needlepoint design consideration. A characteristic Oriental rug design pattern for the needlepoint craftsman has been created to complement the rugs you may own or to enhance any interior. There is a fitting design for any home.

As an additional feature for those who do not wish to mix patterns, and for those who have so often requested something more creative than a matched pair of pillow designs, I have created a series of Designer's Companions, two for each of the three categories. These Companion pieces are not authentic, but are based on authentic Persian patterns. The Companion and the design that inspired it (shown together in the color plates) may be used together or separately. The Companion may be used on any size canvas grid in any size or shape simply by extending or decreasing the pattern graphed.

PLATE 1

Baluchistan
Persian Conventionalized
Prayer Rug Design

The nomadic **Baluchi** tribes of Russia, Afghanistan, and Turkestan settled in the desolate, arid, and sandy southeast corner of Persia known today as Baluchistan. The Baluchi weavings are stylized representations using geometric forms. The octagonal-shaped flower motif characteristically represents a rose, called a gul in Persian. In this case the representation is poor, but the arrangement creates an interesting diagonal look, and the balance of muted colors and stylized design creates a wonderfully soothing effect. Trees of life, symbols of prosperity in Eastern religions, are found in the upper corners in stylized representations. It is interesting to compare this work with the prayer rug designs of the intricate Kashan floral group and the bold Tekke Turkoman geometric example.

This representation of an eighteenth-century Berlin museum piece consists of a 195-by-265-stitch hanging worked on #12 interlocked mono canvas using two strands of 3-ply Persian yarn in shades of gold, pecan, pink, oranges, reds, and blues.

YARN REQUIREMENTS

Light gold	**6 strands**
Medium gold	**6 strands**
Antique gold	**6 strands**
Pecan	**12 strands**
Deep hot pink	**6 strands**
Cherry	**6 strands**
Medium teal	**6 strands**
Navy blue	183 strands
Light tangerine	**12 strands**
Dark tangerine	**12 strands**
Deep pink-orange	**40 strands**
Vermillion	**36 strands**
Deep rust red	**48 strands**

Baluchistan Prayer

Baluchistan Prayer Upper-right Quadrant

▨ Light gold			
▦ Medium gold	▦ Deep hot pink	▦ Navy blue	▦ Deep pink-orange
▦ Antique gold	▦ Cherry	▨ Light tangerine	▨ Vermillion
▦ Pecan	▨ Medium teal	▨ Dark tangerine	■ Deep rust red

13

Baluchistan Prayer Lower-right Quadrant

14

PLATE 2 *(LOWER LEFT)*

Afghan
Central Asiatic Geometric

The influence of the Mongol hordes on the weaving tribes of northern Afghanistan is particularly strong in this design. The Mongols had great appreciation for the handwork of the craftsmen whose lives they spared. The craftsmen, who were forced to migrate to craft centers, created simple, virile, colorful works of art to please their overlords. This bringing together of culturally different craftsmen resulted in the amalgamation of diversified design elements, creating an art that has remained dominant, with little variation, for centuries.

This **Afghan** needlepoint design represents the strong geometry of the nomads. The eight-pointed star, found here and in other Central Asiatic and Caucasian designs, is a nomadic symbol believed to represent the female counterpart of the sun god (represented since earliest times as a circle). The angular, highly geometric floral representation in the border is a naively primitive attempt to incorporate the symbol of eternity (lotus) which is found in the fine arts of all ancient civilizations: Egypt, Mesopotamia, China. . . . The inner design is composed of four identical boxes.

The 234-by-234-stitch square design derived from the Adoros collection was worked on #12 interlocked mono canvas in two strands of 3-ply Persian yarn in typically vivid colors of cranberry, crimson, watermelon, tangerine, and peach on a field of blue-black.

YARN REQUIREMENTS

Cranberry	100 strands
Crimson	63 strands
Watermelon	42 strands
Tangerine	13 strands
Peach	18 strands
Blue-black	210 strands

15

Afghan

Afghan Upper-right Quadrant

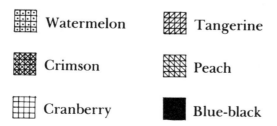

▦ Watermelon	▨ Tangerine
▧ Crimson	▨ Peach
▦ Cranberry	■ Blue-black

PLATE 2 *(UPPER RIGHT)*

Afghan
Designer's Companion

This pattern is a designer's creation; it is not typical of an Afghan total design. Rather, the main border of the characteristic **Afghan** geometric design in Plate 2 has been selected and the stylized, angular, naive floral motif turned into an overall design.

This 150-by-150-stitch square design was worked on #10 interlocked mono canvas with three strands of 3-ply Persian yarn in mulberry, red, watermelon, and pink on a field of midnight blue.

The Designer's Companion can be adapted to a square or rectangle of any size and can be executed on a canvas of any grid size.

YARN REQUIREMENTS

Midnight blue	299 strands
Mulberry	75 strands
Red	87 strands
Watermelon	53 strands
Pink	41 strands

Afghan Designer's Companion

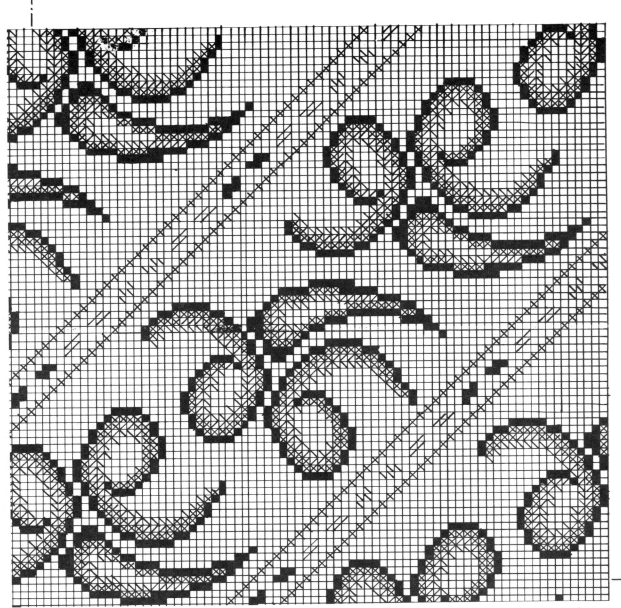

Afghan Designer's Companion Upper-right Quadrant

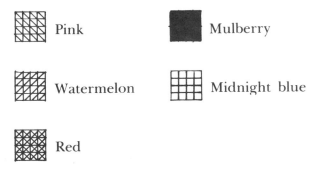

Pink   Mulberry

Watermelon   Midnight blue

Red

PLATE 3 *(UPPER LEFT)*

Bakhtiari
Persian Conventionalized Design

The Persian Bakhtiari tribes live in central Iran south of Isfahan. They are basically nomads, though the older tribesmen remain close to home tending the crops while the younger follow the flocks. The **Bakhtiari** (named for the tribe that created them) are some of the most interesting and beautiful of all the Persian designs. Not only are the designs angular and unconnected, but the colors are bright, gay and bold, reflecting the boldness of nomadic life. They are characterized by two immediately identifiable features uncommon to other Persian designs: distinctive pattern blocks of compartment designs, and use of bright yellows and many shades of green. It is not unusual for the superstitious Bakhtiaris to weave an occasional blue bead into their designs to avoid a curse or ward off the Evil Eye.

This needlepoint design is derived from a modern weaving of a seventeenth-century design in the Montauk collection and is characteristic of the Bakhtiari. This particular piece was woven by Armenians. The single compartment in this design is the same size as in the original carpet. It is a conventionalized floral indicative of the Persian fondness for gardens and the out of doors. The compartment is a replica of one of 51 medallions that cover the field in six rows of six alternating with five rows of three. The design includes conventionalized leaves, unrealistic florals, and a secondary border of the reciprocal trefoil believed to be a symbol of the tree of life. The main border is composed of highly stylized florals. Characteristic of all hand weavings are the irregularities in repeated patterns, variations in dye lots, and an occasional subtle addition or variation to distract the Evil Eye. Note the centers of the anemone florals in the main border.

The 201-by-201-stitch square design was worked on #12 interlocked mono canvas in two strands of 3-ply Persian yarn in old and French blues; black; burgundy and cherry reds; mint; celery and grass greens with pecan; old, medium, light, and pale gold on a field of sea green.

YARN REQUIREMENTS

Old blue	7 strands	Mint green	4 strands	Old gold	47 strands
French blue	13 strands	Celery	2 strands	Medium gold	34 strands
Black	34 strands	Grass green	4 strands	Light gold	18 strands
Burgundy	12 strands	Sea green	92 strands	Pale gold	9 strands
Cherry	12 strands	Pecan	7 strands		

21

Bakhtiari

22

Bakhtiari Upper-right Quadrant

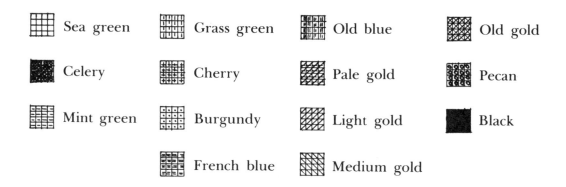

Sea green	Grass green	Old blue	Old gold
Celery	Cherry	Pale gold	Pecan
Mint green	Burgundy	Light gold	Black
	French blue	Medium gold	

23

PLATE 3 *(UPPER RIGHT)*

Kashan
Persian Floral Design

Kashan designs belong to the large family of Persian florals. The realistic floral patterns are well thought out, with intricate arabesques of tendrils, vines, and leaves with flowers that connect in an almost lacelike way. Kashans are characterized by a central medallion and floral corner wedges on a plain field of color. This particular Kashan features a vase in the central medallion surrounded by flowers and vines. The colors are the usual subtle tones of pecan, purples, ivory, blues, greens, and golds that harmoniously complement the intricate design.

This 199-by-199-stitch square design was inspired by a nineteenth-century piece belonging to the Van Alen family. The design was worked on #12 interlocked mono canvas in two strands of 3-ply Persian yarn.

YARN REQUIREMENTS

Ivory	**73 strands**
Pale gold	**27 strands**
Medium gold	**23 strands**
Deep gold	**22 strands**
Pecan	**4 strands**
Mauve	**12 strands**
Pomegranate	**11 strands**
Puce	**16 strands**
Cornflower blue	**10 strands**
French blue	**16 strands**
Sapphire blue	**64 strands**
Celery	**6 strands**
Olive	**6 strands**
Forest green	**6 strands**

Kashan

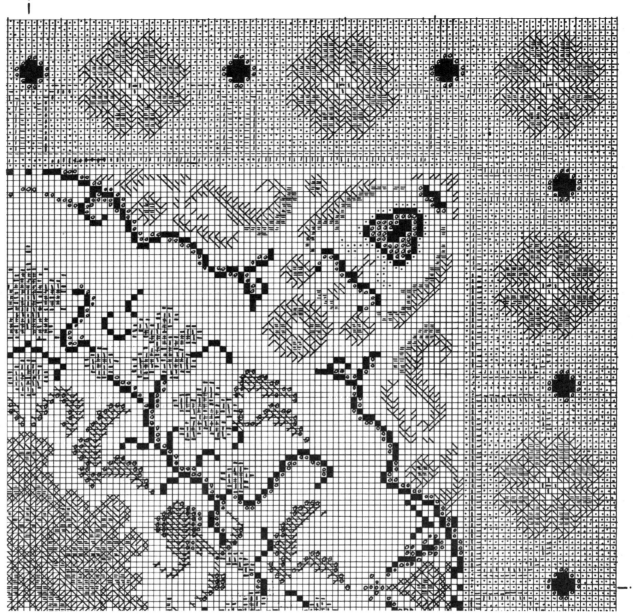

Kashan Upper-right Quadrant

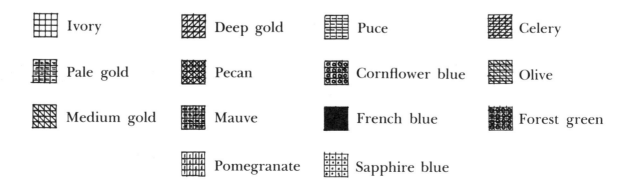

▦ Ivory	▦ Deep gold	▦ Puce	▦ Celery
▦ Pale gold	▦ Pecan	▦ Cornflower blue	▦ Olive
▦ Medium gold	▦ Mauve	■ French blue	▦ Forest green
	▦ Pomegranate	▦ Sapphire blue	

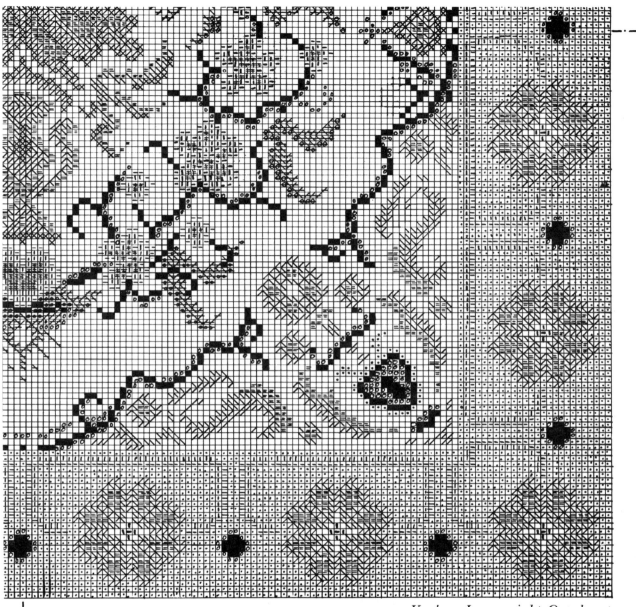

Kashan Lower-right Quadrant

PLATE 3 *(LOWER LEFT)*

Tekke (Khatch)
Central Asiatic Geometric Prayer Rug

This needlepoint design, derived from a nineteenth-century **Tekke** Turkoman prayer rug, is dominated by the boldness of the nomadic tribe geometric design elements and the vivid pure colors so characteristic of Turkoman weaving. The prayer niche, where the worshipper places his forehead while on his hands and knees, is represented as a pointed arch, similar to a mosque portal. Evidence in this original weaving indicates that this rug was also used to hang over an open doorway. A wide, flat, woven selvage on the top where ropes for hanging the rug were attached has been deleted from this design. A subtle cross motif is found in the border surrounding the prayer niche. The Christian cross, called a Khatch in Armenian, is peculiar to Tekke weavings and is evident in the prayer niche itself.

The background is characterized by bold-colored soaring cypress trees of life, symbols of immortality. The geometry almost obscures the boughs and trunks. The "Y" motif of the prayer niche is also a geometric tree configuration.

This 171-by-221-stitch needlepoint representation was worked on #12 interlocked mono canvas with two strands of 3-ply Persian yarn in vibrant colors of gold, tangerine, reds, vermillion, and midnight blue.

YARN REQUIREMENTS

Pale gold	50 strands
Medium gold	30 strands
Deep antique gold	30 strands
Medium tangerine	20 strands
Deep tangerine	20 strands
Vermillion	20 strands
Deep rust red	60 strands
Midnight blue	60 strands

Tekke Prayer

Tekke Prayer Upper-right Quadrant

Pale gold   Medium gold   Deep antique gold   Medium tangerine

Tekke Prayer Lower-right Quadrant

Deep tangerine   Vermillion   Deep rust red   Midnight blue

PLATE 3 *(LOWER RIGHT)*

Kirman
Persian Floral Design

The **Kirman** floral design is perhaps the most popular of all the florals on the American market. Kirman designs not only incorporate the careful delineation of design, a tendency toward realism, and an excellent balance of color and design components, but also characteristically use the softer tones and pastel shades Americans desire. From the early 1920s, more and more pastel weavings were created for export to satisfy American taste.

Persians have always loved the rose and elevated it to the status of the lotus, a symbol of eternity in other Eastern cultures. This particular design of modern origin, belonging to a private collection, illustrates the central floral medallion, floral corner wedges, and wide-banded floral border. The subtle shades are repeated in the medallion and complementary border.

This 191-by-191-stitch square design was worked on #10 interlocked mono canvas in three strands of 3-ply Persian yarn in pale, light, and medium pinks; watermelon; light, medium, and deep taupe; and pale, light, and medium celery greens with olive and forest greens.

YARN REQUIREMENTS

Pale pink	22 strands
Light pink	19 strands
Medium pink	19 strands
Watermelon	19 strands
Light taupe	29 strands
Medium taupe	62 strands
Deep taupe	57 strands
Pale celery	149 strands
Light celery	19 strands
Medium celery	35 strands
Olive	25 strands
Forest green	20 strands

Kirman

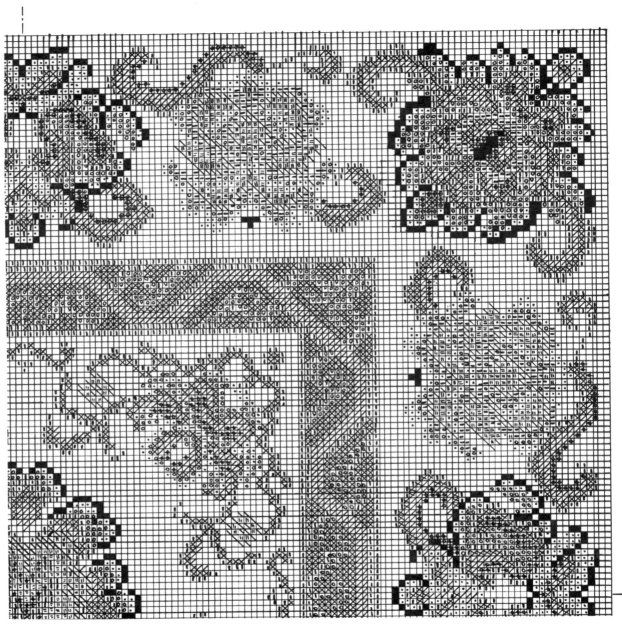

Kirman Upper-right Quadrant

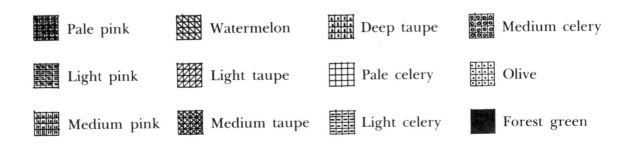

Pale pink

Light pink

Medium pink

Watermelon

Light taupe

Medium taupe

Deep taupe

Pale celery

Light celery

Medium celery

Olive

Forest green

PLATE 4 *(LOWER LEFT)*

Kazak
Caucasian Geometric Design

The **Kazaks** are a nomadic tribe living in the steppes of Central Asia who create the most unconventional of the nomad patterns found in the Caucasus. As with other nomads, there is the tribal fondness for large, bold, angular patterns. The field in a Kazak design is usually divided into three panels that each hold a single figure. The colors are generally vivid and primary. A favorite motif of Kazak design is the latch hook, used in the center of this pattern, which seems to have originated in the Caucasus. Liberal amounts of red, wine, green, and chestnut brown are used in Kazak patterns.

This 167-by-221-stitch rectangular needlepoint design, derived from a modern weaving in the Luther collection, was executed on a #10 interlocked mono canvas with three strands of 3-ply Persian yarn in gold, ivory, cranberry, and warm chestnut brown.

YARN REQUIREMENTS

Ivory	20 strands
Light gold	156 strands
Medium gold	48 strands
Cherry	5 strands
Cranberry	55 strands
Chestnut brown	169 strands

Kazak

Kazak Upper-right Quadrant

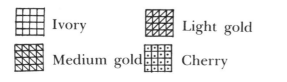 Ivory Light gold Cranberry

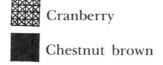 Medium gold Cherry Chestnut brown

37

PLATE 4 *(UPPER RIGHT)*

Kazak
Designer's Companion

The bold, notched geometric figure from the border of the **Kazak** weaving has been used as a dominant design element in this Designer's Companion piece. The angularity of the design is complemented by the use of typical Kazak colorations and conveys the feeling of the bold nomadic Caucasian tribesman of Central Asia.

This 147-by-151-stitch piece was executed on #10 interlocked mono canvas with three strands of 3-ply Persian yarn in medium and deep antique gold, pecan, charcoal brown, pomegranate, and puce.

YARN REQUIREMENTS

Pomegranate	20 strands
Puce	16 strands
Medium gold	40 strands
Deep antique gold	40 strands
Pecan	47 strands
Charcoal brown	107 strands

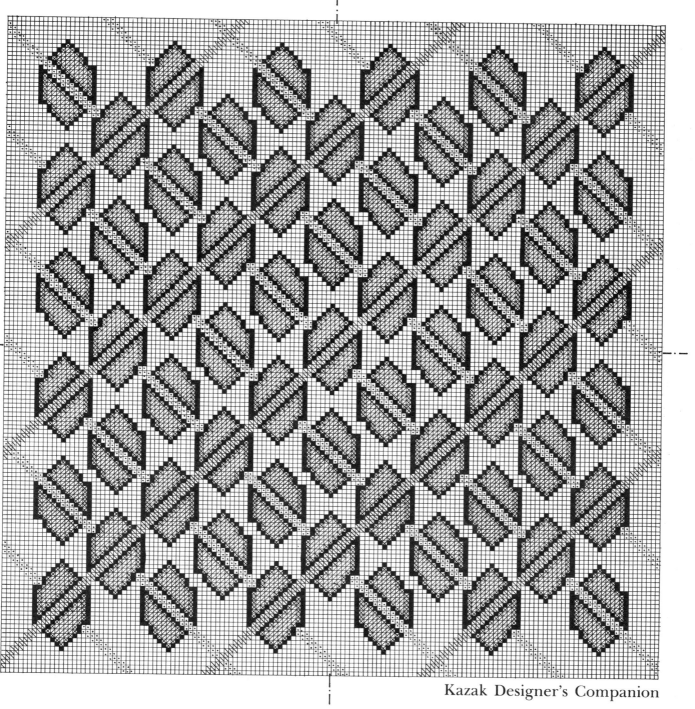

Kazak Designer's Companion

39

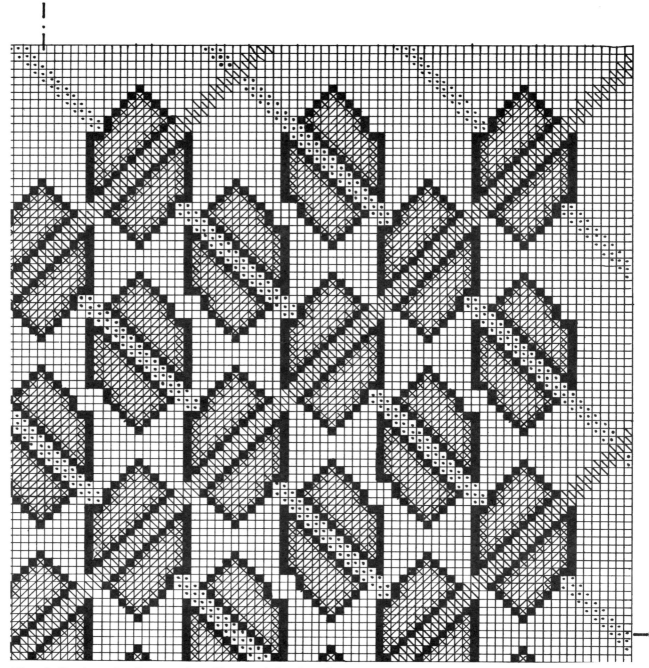

Kazak Designer's Companion Upper-right Quadrant

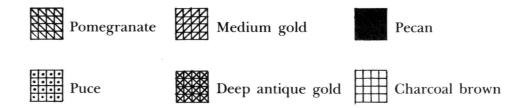

Pomegranate	Medium gold	Pecan
Puce	Deep antique gold	Charcoal brown

PLATE 5 *(LOWER LEFT)*

Herat
Persian Conventionalized Design

Herat, once the capital of the ancient Persian Khorassan Province, is today a city in modern Afghanistan. The Herat weavers developed a pattern that exemplifies the conventionalized design. The pattern is repetitious yet harmonious.

The Herat pattern is most interesting and incorporates the mystical beliefs that have been passed down for centuries. It invariably is composed of a field of rosettes surrounded by two leaves. This is also known as the fish pattern, in which the rosette represents the world, believed to be balanced on the back of a huge turtle. The leaves are fish that chase each other, continuously encircling the world, which makes it rotate, causing day and night. The design is usually bound with several borders. The main border, known as a turtle border, has stylized turtles between Herat rosettes. The colors are simple: reds, blues, and ivories that complement the overall pattern design.

This 207-by-207-stitch square needlepoint design was derived from an antique piece from the Gregorian collection, and was executed on #12 interlocked mono canvas with two strands of 3-ply Persian yarn in ivory; light, medium, and deep antique gold; cornflower, French, and sapphire blues; and pomegranate and puce.

YARN REQUIREMENTS

Ivory cream	**103 strands**
Light gold	**10 strands**
Medium gold	**25 strands**
Deep antique gold	**21 strands**
Pomegranate	**27 strands**
Puce	**30 strands**
Cornflower blue	**15 strands**
French blue	**73 strands**
Sapphire blue	**23 strands**

41

Herat

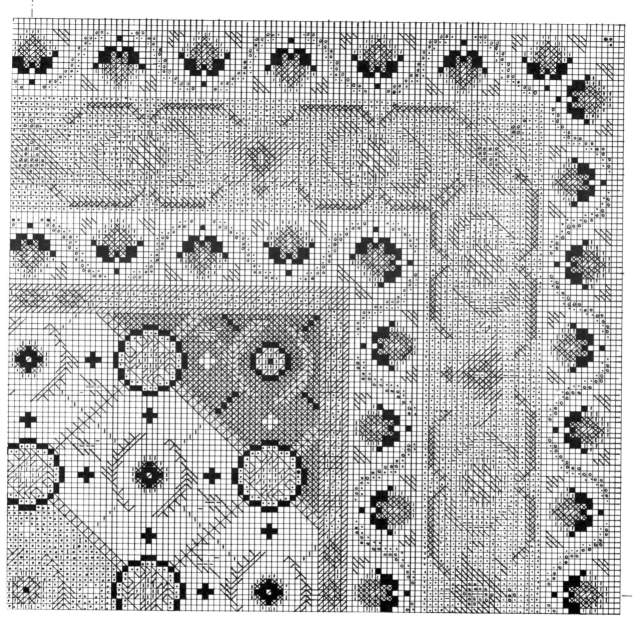

Herat Upper-right Quadrant

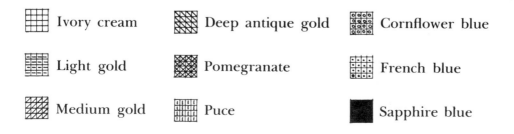

	Ivory cream		Deep antique gold		Cornflower blue
	Light gold		Pomegranate		French blue
	Medium gold		Puce		Sapphire blue

x

43

PLATE 5 *(UPPER RIGHT)*

Herat
Designer's Companion

The uniform repeat of the ancient **Herat** conventionalized design lends itself readily to a modern Designer's Companion. Both the fish design and the turtle border elements have been combined to produce a 160-by-160-stitch square design on #10 interlocked mono canvas using three strands of 3-ply Persian yarn in ivory; medium and deep gold; pecan; cornflower, French, and sapphire blues; and pomegranate and puce.

YARN REQUIREMENTS

Ivory cream	**165 strands**
Medium gold	**18 strands**
Deep antique gold	**12 strands**
Pecan	**5 strands**
Pomegranate	**14 strands**
Puce	**12 strands**
Cornflower blue	**12 strands**
French blue	**11 strands**
Sapphire blue	**19 strands**

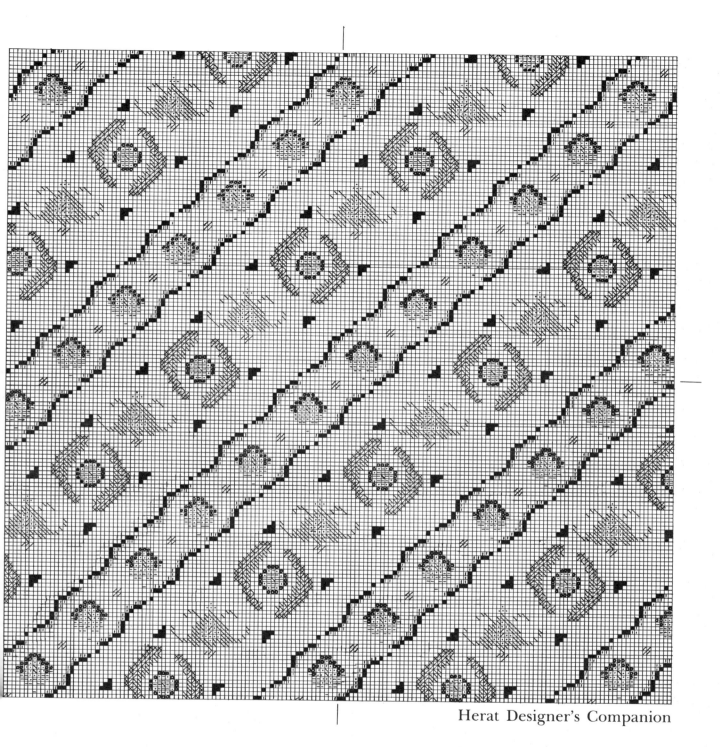

Herat Designer's Companion

45

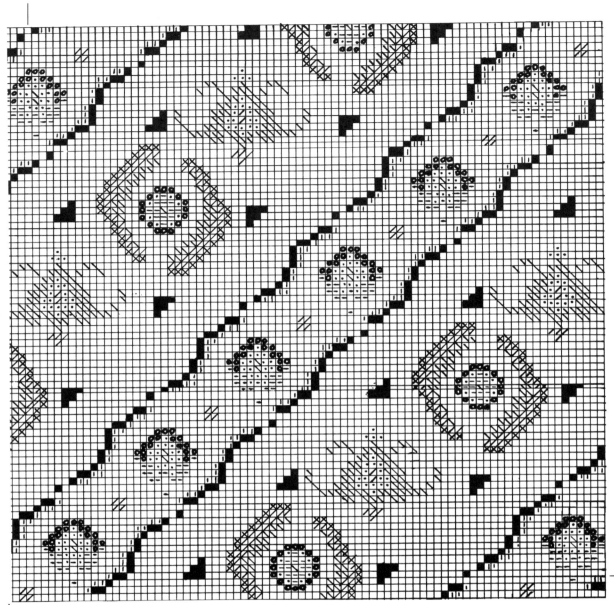

Herat Designer's Companion Upper-right Quadrant

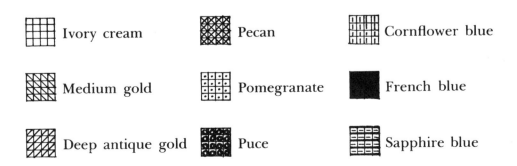

Ivory cream	Pecan	Cornflower blue
Medium gold	Pomegranate	French blue
Deep antique gold	Puce	Sapphire blue

46

PLATE 6

Sarouk
Persian Floral

The **Sarouk** design is one of the most characteristic patterns of the Persian floral group. It is characterized by a central medallion (or concentric medallions) on either a solid field of color or a field lavishly covered with florals. The field is encircled by arabesques that interlace, connect, and form a harmonious whole. Sarouk borders are intricate and derive from the design and colors of the design on the field. Sarouks with the floral field have been extremely popular with the American buyer since Victorian times. The typical Sarouk colorations and floral design blended well with the bric-a-brac and fretwork fussiness of Victorian rooms. More recently the newer Sarouks with plain fields have gained preeminence on the market.

This needlepoint design is a typical floral Sarouk in which the field of deep coral is completely covered with connected florals about a central medallion that almost totally blends into the patterns surrounding it. The field design is set off by a quasigeometric border in tones taken from the field design. The main border is dominant in design and size, utilizing color and form from the field. This border emphasizes the scroll and arabesque nature of florals; the deep blue-black tone of the surrounding field further accentuates the delicate flowing line. Solid color bands on the outside contribute to the intricacy of the main border.

This 179-by-179-stitch square Sarouk design of the early twentieth century was worked on #12 interlocked mono canvas with two strands of 3-ply Persian yarn in ivory, midnight blue, turquoise, medium and deep gold, and medium and deep coral. The design belongs to the collection of Mr. and Mrs. Charles Churnin.

YARN REQUIREMENTS

Midnight blue	70 strands
Turquoise	20 strands
Deep gold	5 strands
Medium gold	12 strands
Deep coral	35 strands
Medium coral	15 strands
Ivory	40 strands

Sarouk

Sarouk Upper-right Quadrant

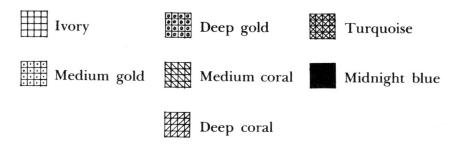

Ivory

Medium gold

Deep gold

Medium coral

Deep coral

Turquoise

Midnight blue

PLATE 7 *(UPPER LEFT)*

Afghan
Central Asiatic Design

The Central Asiatic **Afghan** weavings are not actually in the Turkoman group, although they are very similar to those made by the Bokhara family of weavers. They are typically nomads' geometrics. Within the Afghan group there is a strong conformity of design that shows the strongest influence of the Mongols. This design tradition has been passed down since the 1500s by tribes living in northern Afghanistan. The characteristic motif is the octagonal rose figure—the gul.

This Afghan needlepoint design features one gul (the same size as in the original carpet) that is repeated in four unconnected rows of eight guls each. The original carpet design dates back to the sixteenth century. The gul has an open field center, with characteristic nomads' geometry in the four quarters. One of four secondary guard stripes (borders) is characteristically a modification of a central theme motif.

This 191-by-191-stitch square design of the Berlin Adoros collection has been worked on #10 interlocked mono canvas in three strands of 3-ply Persian yarn in pure, intense colors: blue-black, crimson, cherry, and hot pink.

YARN REQUIREMENTS

Blue-black	86 strands
Crimson	186 strands
Cherry	29 strands
Hot pink	27 strands

Afghan

51

Afghan Upper-right Quadrant

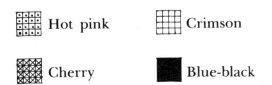

Hot pink   Crimson

Cherry   Blue-black

PLATE 7 *(UPPER RIGHT)*

Baluchistan
Persian Conventionalized Design

The nomadic tribes of **Baluchistan** in bleak southeast Persia weave some very interesting conventionalized patterns reflecting their heritage of strong geometric forms. The gul, or eight-sided rose figure, is a typical representation. In this case it has been adorned with highly stylized floral arrangements within the sectors. The colors tend to be somber and muted. The gul represented in this needlepoint design is only one of many seen in the original nineteenth-century piece, in which guls were arranged in vertical and horizontal rows surrounded by a series of minor stripes and one main border.

This 150-by-150-stitch square representation was worked on #10 interlocked mono canvas in three strands of 3-ply Persian yarn in pale, medium, and deep pink-oranges; vermillion, rust red, hot pink, and cranberry; and shades of gold on a sapphire blue background.

YARN REQUIREMENTS

Pale pink-orange	6 strands
Medium pink-orange	15 strands
Deep pink-orange	16 strands
Vermillion	20 strands
Deep rust red	48 strands
Hot pink	20 strands
Cranberry	16 strands
Pale gold	7 strands
Medium gold	7 strands
Deep antique gold	10 strands
Sapphire blue	136 strands

Baluchistan

Baluchistan Upper-right Quadrant

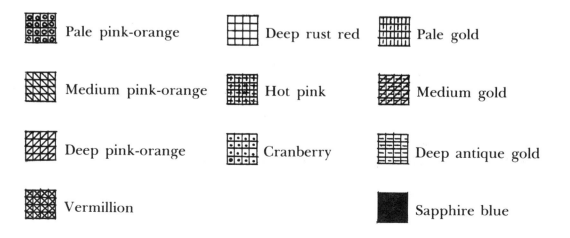

Pale pink-orange

Medium pink-orange

Deep pink-orange

Vermillion

Deep rust red

Hot pink

Cranberry

Pale gold

Medium gold

Deep antique gold

Sapphire blue

PLATE 7 *(LOWER LEFT)*

Bijar
Persian Floral Design

This circular floral needlepoint representation was derived from a **Bijar** weaving of the nineteenth century, now in the Luther Collection. The circular form comes from the central medallion motif; borders have been eliminated to emphasize the delicate floral motif, which uses pine cones, florals, and leaves. The delineations are bold; the colors are vivid; the outlining and dividing lines are severe and lack the delicate refinement of other Persian florals, but the piece is no less beautiful. The serrated leaf motif indicates the strong Kurdish influence.

The circular design has a diameter of 175 stitches and was worked on a #12 interlocked mono canvas with two strands of 3-ply Persian yarn in ivory; light, medium, and deep gold; ice, cornflower, French, sapphire, and midnight blues; deep pink-orange, vermillion, and deep rust red.

YARN REQUIREMENTS

Ivory	6 strands
Light gold	23 strands
Medium gold	13 strands
Deep gold	22 strands
Ice blue	14 strands
Cornflower blue	8 strands
French blue	10 strands
Sapphire blue	6 strands
Midnight blue	64 strands
Deep pink-orange	8 strands
Vermillion	8 strands
Deep rust red	18 strands

Bijar

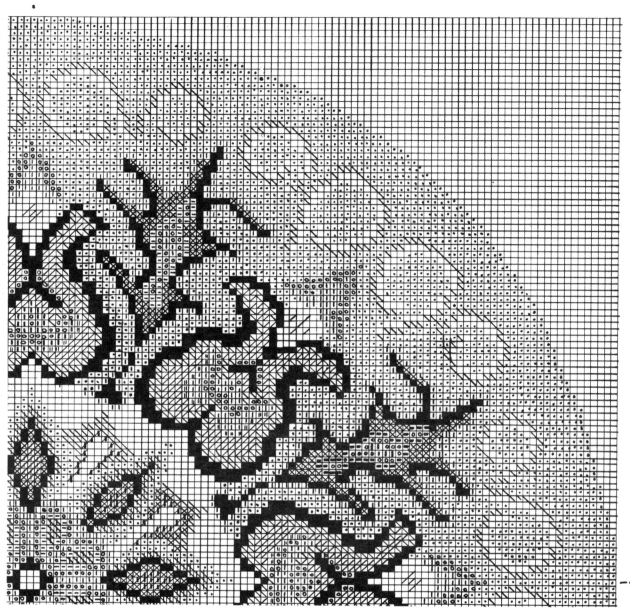

Bijar Upper-right Quadrant

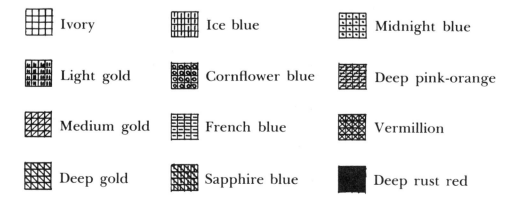

⊞ Ivory	⊞ Ice blue	⊞ Midnight blue
⊞ Light gold	⊞ Cornflower blue	⊞ Deep pink-orange
⊞ Medium gold	⊞ French blue	⊞ Vermillion
⊞ Deep gold	⊞ Sapphire blue	■ Deep rust red

PLATE 7 *(LOWER RIGHT)*

Bijar
Persian Conventionalized Design

There are two distinct types of **Bijars:** those woven by the very poor Persians of the village of Bijar proper in Azerbaijan Province, and those Kurdish Bijars woven by the Kurdish tribes living in the little villages surrounding the town. The Kurdish Bijars tend to be conventionalized design patterns combining the best techniques and designs of the Persians and Kurds into a unique style with distinctive masses of vivid, strong colors. Perhaps due to the bleakness of the terrain and the Kurdish tradition, the more subtle Persian hues have been replaced by the brighter colors of Asia Minor. The patterns are basically plain, unpretentious, and conservative. The designs are straightforward and comfortable to live with.

This needlepoint representation copies the central medallion motif with highly stylized floral wedge corners on a field of vivid sapphire blue. There is an unusual combination of yellow-golds and terra-cottas.

The 187-by-215-stitch design was worked on #10 interlocked mono canvas with three strands of 3-ply Persian yarn in shades of blue, pink-orange, terra-cotta, gold, and ivory.

YARN REQUIREMENTS

Light pink-orange	8 strands
Medium pink-orange	20 strands
Deep pink-orange	73 strands
Vermillion	44 strands
Deep rust red	20 strands
Hot pink	5 strands
Cranberry	12 strands
Ivory	90 strands
Medium gold	13 strands
Deep antique gold	48 strands
Pecan	6 strands
Cornflower blue	15 strands
Sapphire blue	144 strands

Bijar

60

Bijar Upper-right Quadrant

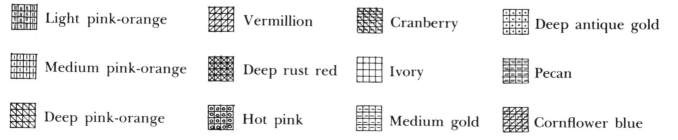

Light pink-orange

Vermillion

Cranberry

Deep antique gold

Medium pink-orange

Deep rust red

Ivory

Pecan

Deep pink-orange

Hot pink

Medium gold

Cornflower blue

Sapphire blue

PLATE 8 *(LOWER LEFT)*

Bijar
Persian Floral Design

The Persians of Bijar village have been strongly influenced by the Kurds, who once invaded the area and later settled in the villages surrounding the town. The subtle tones of typical Persian florals have given way to bold, vibrant colorations. Although the **Bijar** workings of floral patterns tend to be bold and primitive, many patterns rival the typical florals of Kashan and Sarouk. The major differences lie in the weaving and chosen colors. Bijars exhibit the greatest latitude of pattern design, using overall florals, central medallion motifs, and patterns that flow over and pierce intricate borders. The weavings are characterized by abundant uses of yellows, greens, and terra-cottas.

This needlepoint representation of a weaving in the Luther Collection incorporates the use of the overall floral pattern piercing the intricate border. There is a wonderful juxtaposition of vivid colors accentuating the individual floral elements. This 210-by-210-stitch square design was worked on #14 interlocked mono canvas in many shades of blue, pink-orange, terra-cotta, gold, and ivory. The 44,100 stitches of this 15-inch-square piece use two strands of 3-ply Persian yarn.

YARN REQUIREMENTS

Cornflower blue	9 strands
French blue	12 strands
Sapphire blue	6 strands
Navy blue	97 strands
Ivory	50 strands
Light gold	20 strands
Medium gold	12 strands
Deep antique gold	32 strands
Vermillion	18 strands
Deep rust red	14 strands
Light pink-orange	6 strands
Medium pink-orange	16 strands
Dark pink-orange	15 strands
Hot pink	6 strands
Cherry	6 strands

Bijar

63

Bijar Upper-right Quadrant

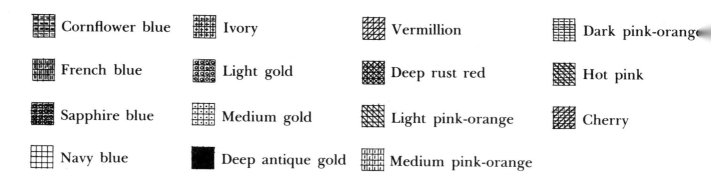

Cornflower blue	Ivory	Vermillion	Dark pink-orange
French blue	Light gold	Deep rust red	Hot pink
Sapphire blue	Medium gold	Light pink-orange	Cherry
Navy blue	Deep antique gold	Medium pink-orange	

PLATE 8 *(UPPER RIGHT)*

Bijar
Designer's Companion

This needlepoint Designer's Companion was derived from the floral type of **Bijar,** using floral elements from the intricate field design combined with the elements found in the border. The vivid colors typical of all Bijars have been used to create a pattern and coloration which, when used as a companion with the floral Bijar, complements and enhances the more intricate detail of the floral. The simplicity of the Designer's Companion is certainly consistent with Bijar design.

The 150-by-150-stitch square Designer's Companion was worked on #10 interlocked mono canvas with three strands of 3-ply Persian yarn in medium and deep pink-orange; vermillion; deep rust red; hot pink; cherry; ivory; medium and deep antique golds; and cornflower, French, sapphire, and navy blues.

YARN REQUIREMENTS

Medium pink-orange	6 strands
Deep pink-orange	6 strands
Vermillion	5 strands
Deep rust red	6 strands
Hot pink	6 strands
Cherry	7 strands
Ivory	155 strands
Medium gold	11 strands
Deep antique gold	17 strands
Cornflower blue	10 strands
French blue	17 strands
Sapphire blue	12 strands
Navy blue	10 strands

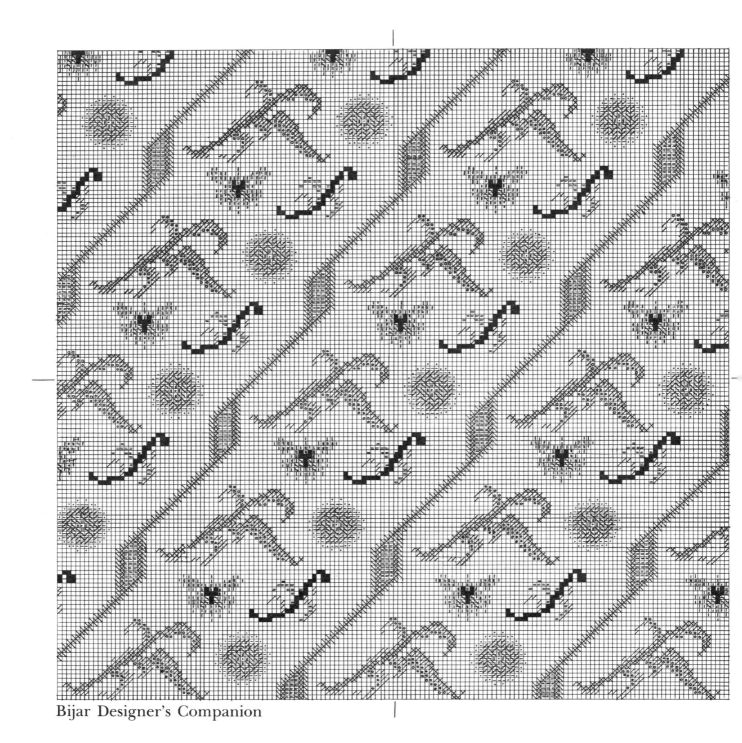

Bijar Designer's Companion

66

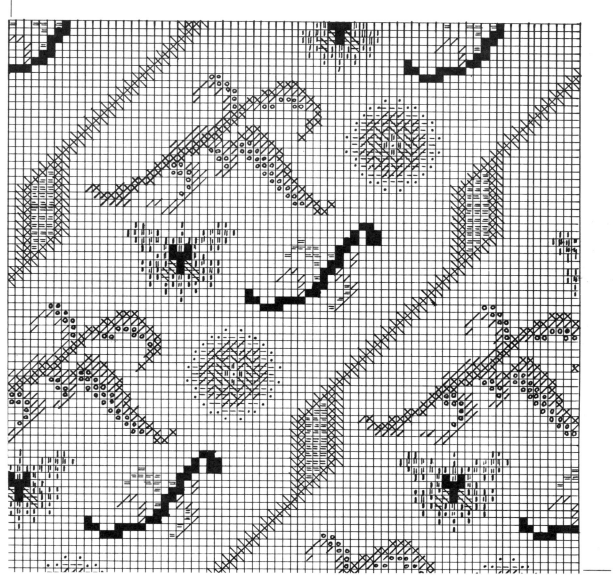

Bijar Designer's Companion Upper-right Quadrant

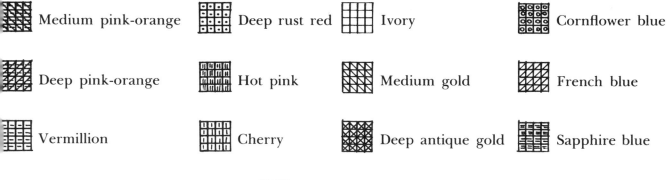

Medium pink-orange

Deep pink-orange

Vermillion

Deep rust red

Hot pink

Cherry

Ivory

Medium gold

Deep antique gold

Cornflower blue

French blue

Sapphire blue

Navy blue

PLATE 9 (*LOWER RIGHT*)

Tabriz
Persian Conventionalized Design

The city of Tabriz, once the capital of Persia, is in the northwesternmost part of Iran, closest to Russia. Tabriz, now the capital of Azerbaijan Province, has been since earliest times a major trade center. Due to cultural interchange, the designs of Tabriz vary greatly from florals to conventionalized patterns. This needlepoint example of **Tabriz** design is typical of the repetitive yet harmonious design, decidedly different from the nomads' geometrics and the detailed florals. Many designs are copies or interpretations of the mosaics of the mosques of Tabriz.

This design is derived from a modern weaving done under the aegis of the Taba Tabai family, who were known for using classical sixteenth- and seventeenth-century patterns. The design has a jewel-like mosaic quality. The simple nonrealistic compartment design is pleasing. The basic pattern was repeated many times on the field. The four borders are repeated in reverse order, creating the effect of one main border. The stylized floral medallions appear to be tied together by the inner two guard stripes and sawtooth motif.

The 179-by-179-stitch square design was worked on #12 interlocked mono canvas with two strands of 3-ply Persian yarn in pecan; old, medium, and light golds; and two shades of Tabriz blue—a favorite color in these weavings, named after the tiles of the Blue Mosque of Tabriz.

YARN REQUIREMENTS

Old gold	22 strands
Medium gold	33 strands
Light gold	33 strands
Pecan	16 strands
Deep Tabriz blue	64 strands
Medium Tabriz blue	9 strands

Tabriz

69

Tabriz Upper-right Quadrant

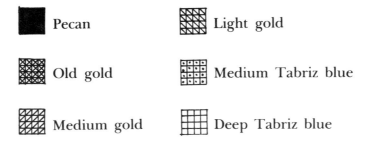

	Pecan		Light gold
	Old gold		Medium Tabriz blue
	Medium gold		Deep Tabriz blue

PLATE 9 *(UPPER LEFT)*

Tabriz
Designer's Companion

The city of **Tabriz** has been the home of many Turks for centuries. Although these Turks are Persians, they are descendants of the Seljuks and are Turkic speaking. The influences of Persian design are strong, yet traces of the Turkish geometric designs still surface. These are not at all unsympathetic with the conventionalized representations of the mosque mosaics.

This Designer's Companion is characterized by the four borders, used in reverse order to create what appears to be a wide band encompassing stylized anemone medallions. The finished canvas can be of any size if you establish your own rectangular or square dimensions and use the graphic delineation I have designed for this 144-by-144-stitch square design on #10 interlocked mono canvas using three strands of 3-ply Persian yarns in pecan; deep, medium, light, and pale golds; and medium Tabriz blue on a field of deep Tabriz blue.

YARN REQUIREMENTS

Deep gold	18 strands
Medium gold	16 strands
Light gold	15 strands
Pale gold	15 strands
Pecan	8 strands
Deep Tabriz blue	195 strands
Medium Tabriz blue	7 strands

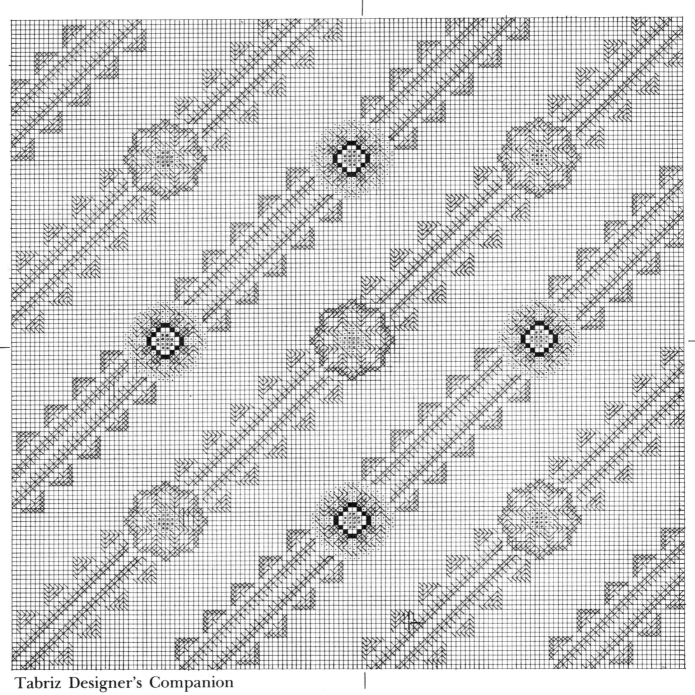

Tabriz Designer's Companion

72

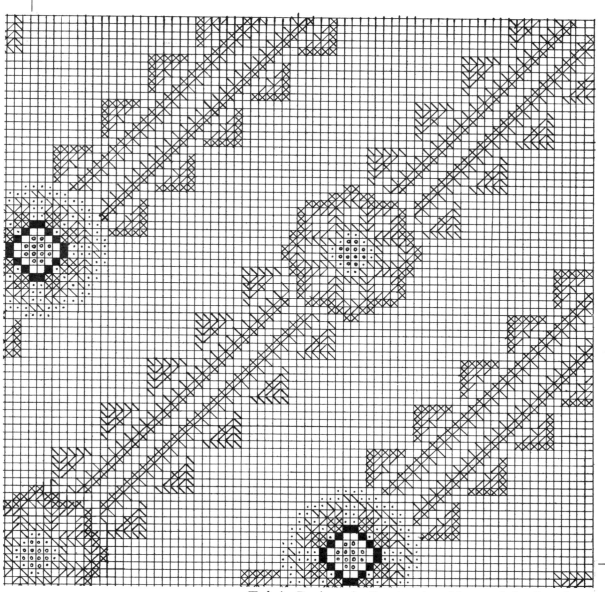

Tabriz Designer's Companion Upper-right Quadrant

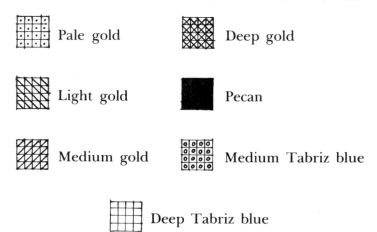

Pale gold

Deep gold

Light gold

Pecan

Medium gold

Medium Tabriz blue

Deep Tabriz blue

PLATE 10 *(LOWER RIGHT)*

Sarouk
Persian Floral

When a design is truly floral—incorporating flowers, buds, vines, tendrils, leaves, and perhaps a vase in an intricate design—with a tendency toward realism, and its elements are interlaced, scrolled, and connected, it is undoubtedly Persian. Floral patterns suggest the sedentary, philosophical, educated, planned life that is so different from the more virile, harsh, unstable nomadic life. The well-drawn, well-thought-out designs may incorporate up to seven borders, which are coordinated with the design of the field. There is a balance of parts and colors. **Sarouk** floral designs are most often characterized by large central medallions with pendants, or by two or more concentric medallions, on a solid field set off from the four corners by two or three rows of solid color (lines). The borders are usually characterized by a wide main border of vines and flowers reminiscent of the central motif. Secondary borders are used to emphasize the main border and are executed with the greatest latitude of design. Typical field colors are blue, rose, and shades of red and coral.

This Sarouk floral needlepoint design utilizes a typical central medallion, emphasized by the deep-blue arabesque circular design on an ivory background, with corner wedges of floral clusters. The main floral border, on a deep-blue field drawn from the central medallion, picks up on the pattern and colors of the central motif and is emphasized by the rigidity of reverse sawtooth borders on each edge. A favorite Persian design, the Shah Abbas—named for the early-seventeenth-century ruler who brought eminence to his capital of Isfahan as a cultural center—is the central motif on each side of the main border. Though each border design of the five-border band varies greatly with the design of the central motif, each one is emphasized by the use of the medallion colors creating a typically intricate, harmonious Sarouk design.

This eighteenth-century Sarouk needlepoint design, from a weaving in the Churnin collection, has been worked on #12 interlocked mono canvas with two strands of 3-ply Persian yarn. The 227-by-227-stitch square design uses colors of garnet, coral, medium coral, and peach; deep, medium, pale, and light golds; midnight, old, French, and light blues on a central field of ivory.

YARN REQUIREMENTS

Garnet	63 strands	Deep gold	22 strands	Old blue	30 strands
Coral	9 strands	Medium gold	26 strands	French blue	15 strands
Medium coral	6 strands	Very light gold	23 strands	Light blue	8 strands
Peach	6 strands	Pale gold	18 strands	Ivory	46 strands
		Midnight blue	119 strands		

Sarouk

Sarouk Upper-right Quadrant

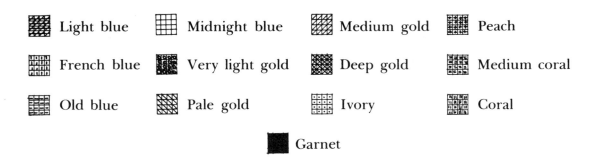

Light blue	Midnight blue	Medium gold	Peach
French blue	Very light gold	Deep gold	Medium coral
Old blue	Pale gold	Ivory	Coral
	Garnet		

PLATE 10 *(UPPER LEFT)*

Sarouk
Designer's Companion

This Designer's Companion to the Sarouk Persian floral design takes as its theme a floral element typical of the **Sarouk** designs. The triple floral element from the main border of the Sarouk Persian floral design is worked on the bias here, and is connected by vines and tendrils. This Designer's Companion may be worked as a rectangle or a square.

This 140-by-140-stitch square companion was worked on #10 interlocked mono canvas with three strands of 3-ply Persian yarn in light, medium, and deep antique gold; ice, cornflower, French, and sapphire blues; medium and deep pink-orange; vermillion and deep rust red.

YARN REQUIREMENTS

Light gold	18 strands
Medium gold	18 strands
Deep antique gold	13 strands
Ice blue	10 strands
Cornflower blue	25 strands
French blue	12 strands
Sapphire blue	106 strands
Medium pink-orange	3 strands
Deep pink-orange	3 strands
Vermillion	10 strands
Deep rust red	18 strands

Sarouk Designer's Companion

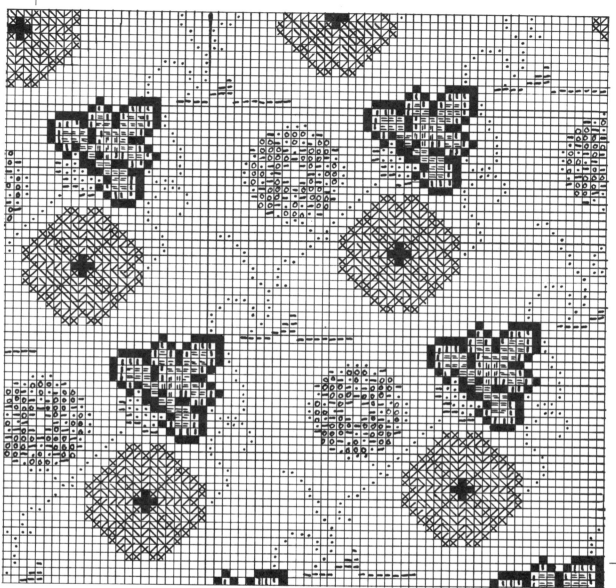

Sarouk Designer's Companion Upper-right Quadrant

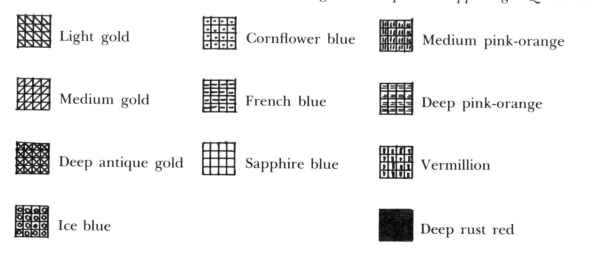

Light gold	Cornflower blue	Medium pink-orange
Medium gold	French blue	Deep pink-orange
Deep antique gold	Sapphire blue	Vermillion
Ice blue		Deep rust red

PLATE 11 *(LOWER RIGHT)*

Khiva Bokhara
Central Asiatic Geometric

Of all Persian and Oriental rug designs, the Central Asiatic group adheres more strictly to a uniform pattern of design and color than any other group. The classical and most well-known **Bokhara** pattern design of the Turkoman tribes was originally produced by nomads who roamed east of the Caspian Sea and to the north of present-day Iran. The Turkomans are the cultural and ethnic descendants of the Mongolian hordes that conquered Central Asia from the twelfth through the fifteenth centuries. The pattern derives its name from the city of Bokhara, which was in northern Persia (now Soviet Turkestan) where the tribesmen brought their crafts to market. The Bokhara pattern is characteristically woven by Yomud, Tekke, and Khiva tribesmen as well as by Armenians. Today the classical patterns come from Iran, Afghanistan, and Russia.

Bokharas are characterized by the octagonal motif sometimes called the elephant foot or gul (rose) in Persian. (The gul is represented always by an octagonal figure.) The colors are pure and bold: predominantly deep red, deep blue, and ivory or white, with shades of coral, rose, pink, and orange. The octagons may be large or small, geometrically perfect or elongated, placed in contact in perpendicular rows or separated by diamonds or other geometric shapes in between.

This Khiva Bokhara needlepoint design is the classical, well-known Bokhara example from the collection of Mitchell Levine. There is a series of separated, quartered guls in the main field, in a deep cranberry color. Characteristic geometric motifs fill the open spaces between them. The main border and guard stripes (secondary borders) are typically pure nomads' simple geometric designs. The 151-by-177-stitch rectangular design has been worked in #10 interlocked mono canvas with three strands of 3-ply Persian yarns of midnight blue, cranberry, crimson, watermelon, pink, and white.

REQUIREMENTS

Midnight blue	76 strands
Deep cranberry	134 strands
White	2 strands
Crimson	20 strands
Watermelon	41 strands
Pink	16 strands

Khiva Bokhara

Khiva Bokhara Upper-right Quadrant

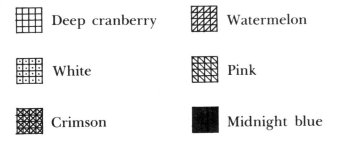

⊞ Deep cranberry   ▨ Watermelon

▦ White   ▤ Pink

▨ Crimson   ■ Midnight blue

82

PLATE 11 *(LOWER LEFT)*

Saraband
Persian Conventionalized Design

The Persian **Saraband** is a typical conventionalized design with an overall field pattern that is repetitious, soothing, and harmonious. Of all Persian designs, no other has remained unaltered from the earliest times to the present. The main design element is the almond nut, known as a cone, pineapple, palm top, or pear design. Due to migrations and cross-cultural influences, the almond nut design developed the greatest number of variations and is found in the weavings of Persia, Turkestan, the Caucasus, and Asia Minor. The plain field is covered with the nut design arranged in transverse rows, with the smaller ends of the nut pointing in opposite directions in alternating rows. The characteristic borders are long and angular. The field color is usually blue, red, or ivory. If the field is blue, the nut is red; if the field is red, the nut is blue; if the field is ivory, the nut is red or blue. The blues are deep and rich tones; reds are mellow.

This 190-by-180-stitch needlepoint design was derived from a classical museum piece and was worked on #10 interlocked mono canvas with three strands of 3-ply Persian yarn in ivory; navy; light, medium, and deep gold; celery and mint greens; with cherry and cranberry reds.

YARN REQUIREMENTS

Navy blue	88 strands
Ivory	59 strands
Light gold	52 strands
Medium gold	26 strands
Deep gold	24 strands
Cherry	87 strands
Cranberry	21 strands
Celery	10 strands
Mint green	10 strands

Saraband

84

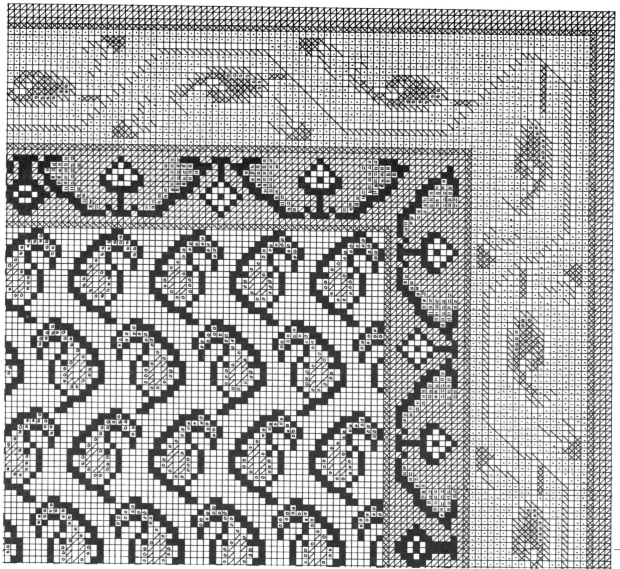

Saraband Upper-right Quadrant

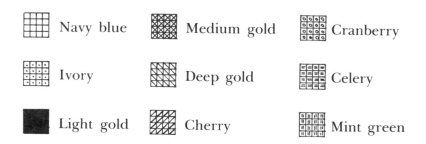

	Navy blue		Medium gold		Cranberry
	Ivory		Deep gold		Celery
	Light gold		Cherry		Mint green

PLATE 11 *(UPPER RIGHT)*

Ganja
Caucasian Geometric Design

Caucasian rugs can be divided into three groups: Kazak, Georgian, and Armenian. Most Caucasian rugs are from Armenia, an ancient country bounded by Russia, Turkey, Persia, and the Black and Caspian seas.

Tribes of mixed origin wandered between Lakes Gotcha, Van, and Urumiah in Caucasia, Armenia, and Persia. Their stopping-off place for trade was Elizabethpol, known as **Ganja** when it was ruled by Persia. Hence, the rugs they marketed acquired the name Ganja.

The Armenians were converted to Christianity in the fourth century. Although they were conquered and absorbed by Islamic peoples, they held tight to their faith. Very often the Christian cross is visible in their weavings, even finding its way into Islamic prayer rugs. A cross in one of these is a subtle clue indicating the weaver was Armenian. The designs are geometric and usually outlined in a complementary color of blue, green, tan, coral, or gold. Stylized trees with extended branches are a typical pattern woven to produce a diagonal effect. This Ganja design very closely resembles a Kazak pattern and undoubtedly was woven by an Armenian because of the Christian symbols, trees, and diagonal effect.

This 159-by-159-stitch square needlepoint representation was worked on #10 interlocked mono canvas in three strands of 3-ply Persian yarn in cornflower, sapphire, and navy blues; celery and mint greens, with cherry and cranberry; and light, medium, and deep golds.

YARN REQUIREMENTS

Cornflower blue	5 strands
Sapphire blue	6 strands
Navy blue	113 strands
Light gold	34 strands
Medium gold	15 strands
Deep gold	25 strands
Cherry	81 strands
Cranberry	25 strands
Celery	4 strands
Mint green	5 strands

Ganja

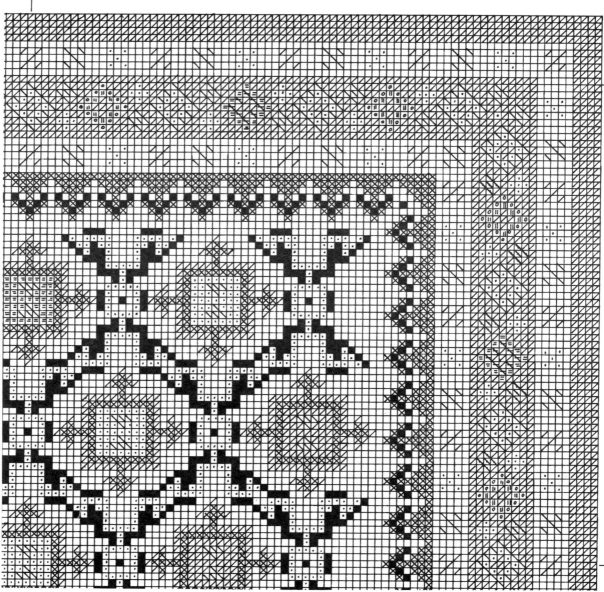

Ganja Upper-right Quadrant

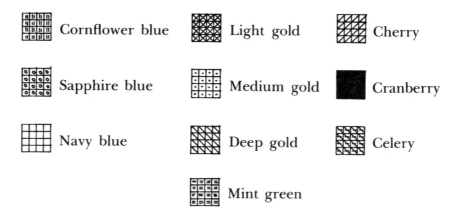

Cornflower blue	Light gold	Cherry
Sapphire blue	Medium gold	Cranberry
Navy blue	Deep gold	Celery
	Mint green	

PLATE 11 *(UPPER LEFT)*

Tekke Bokhara
Central Asiatic Geometric

This **Bokhara** needlepoint design was selected to illustrate not only the characteristic gul, but also the slight variations incorporated by the Tekke weaving family of the Turkoman tribes. With the czarist crackdown on the nomads in 1881, some Tekke tribes migrated south to northern Iran to live in their traditional ways. They continue to be nomadic and produce the characteristic Bokhara pattern. The Tekkes create meticulous patterns with an exquisite use of the gul and with small geometric border designs that are not at all related to the design of the field.

This needlepoint design derives from a late nineteenth-century weaving owned by Mitchell Levine and incorporates only four of the many somewhat elongated quartered guls of the original. These are placed on an open field of cranberry and are separated by small geometrics. The guard and main borders reflect the more intricate geometric designs of the Tekkes and are unrelated to the design motif of the field.

This 165-by-229-stitch horizontally rectangular needlepoint design is worked on #12 interlocked mono canvas in two strands of 3-ply Persian yarn in white, midnight blue, cranberry, crimson, and watermelon.

YARN REQUIREMENTS

Midnight blue	42 strands
White	8 strands
Cranberry	112 strands
Crimson	41 strands
Watermelon	12 strands

89

Tekke Bokhara

Tekke Bokhara Upper-right Quadrant

 White

 Crimson

 Watermelon

Cranberry

 Midnight blue

91

PLATE 12

Kashan
Persian Floral Prayer Rug Design

It is interesting to note that within each subgroup of Oriental rug design (geometric, conventionalized, floral), excellent examples of each style are found in the prayer rug designs. The characteristics exhibited by each group are consistent. As one would expect, the **Kashan** prayer rug shows the great beauty of detail and well-thought-out balance of floral design elements indicative of all Kashans.

In this case, the prayer niche is intricate and takes on a scroll-like effect, with curved flowing lines characteristic of the mosque domes and portals. Blossoming trees and the tree of life decorate the prayer niche, which is surrounded by an overall floral background.

This 139-by-179-stitch needlepoint piece was inspired by an antique museum piece and was worked on #12 interlocked mono canvas in two strands of 3-ply Persian yarn in shades of gold and tones of blue, pecan, pink, orange, and red.

YARN REQUIREMENTS

Pale gold	62 strands
Medium gold	12 strands
Deep antique gold	12 strands
Pecan	8 strands
Medium pink-orange	8 strands
Hot pink	11 strands
Ice blue	6 strands
Cornflower blue	6 strands
French blue	18 strands
Sapphire blue	12 strands
Midnight blue	32 strands
Cherry	18 strands
Cranberry	34 strands

Kashan Prayer

Kashan Prayer Upper-right Quadrant

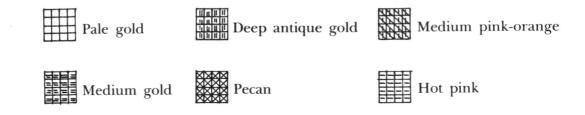

Pale gold   Deep antique gold   Medium pink-orange

Medium gold   Pecan   Hot pink

94

Kashan Prayer Lower-right Quadrant

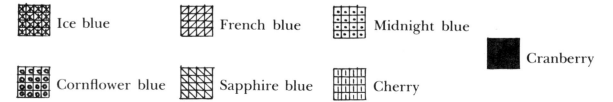

Ice blue   French blue   Midnight blue

Cornflower blue   Sapphire blue   Cherry

Cranberry

95

DATE DUE